The Stamp Act Crisis

1765-1766

By Jack E. Fryar, Jr.

The Young Reader's Series of North Carolina History
from
Dram Tree Books

Designed for parents, teachers, home schoolers, or anyone else looking for a fun, informative way to start teaching children about the rich, colorful history of the Tar Heel State. These books use historic photographs and illustrations, original artwork, and simple but engaging narrative to introduce youngsters to history in a fun way!

Copyright © 2025 by Jack E. Fryar, Jr.
All rights reserved. No part of this book may be reproduced in any form or by any electronic or mechanical means, including information storage and retrieval systems, without written permission from the publisher, except by a reviewer who may quote brief passages in a review.
First Edition 2025
Published in the United States of America by Dram Tree Books

Discounts available for educators. Call or email for terms:
(910) 538-4076
dramtreebooks@gmail.com

Publisher's Cataloging-in-Publication Data (Provided by DRT Press, Inc.):
Names: Fryar, Jack E., author.
Title: The Stamp Act crisis , 1765-1766 / by Jack E. Fryar, Jr.
Series: The Young Readers Series of North Carolina History
Description: Wilmington, NC: Dram Tree Books, 2025. | Summary: A recount of the Stamp Act Crisis, North Carolina's early rebellion against British taxation, highlighting armed resistance in Wilmington that blocked stamp deliveries—years before the Boston Tea Party and earning the state's "First in Freedom" legacy.
Identifiers: ISBN: 978-0-9844900-8-0
Subjects: LCSH Great Britain. Stamp Act (1765)--Juvenile literature. | North Carolina--History--Revolution, 1775-1783. | Taxation--Political aspects--United States--History--18th century--Juvenile literature. | Protest movements--United States--History--18th century--Juvenile literature. | Riots--United States--History--18th century--Juvenile literature. | United States--History--Colonial period, ca. 1600-1775--Juvenile literature. | United States--History--Revolution, 1775-1783--Causes--Juvenile literature. | Great Britain--Relations--United States--Juvenile literature. | United States--Relations--Great Britain--Juvenile literature. | BISAC JUVENILE NONFICTION / History / United States / Colonial & Revolutionary
Classification: LCC E215.2 .F79 2025 | DDC 973.2/7--dc23

Dram Tree Books • P.O. Box 7183 • Wilmington, N.C. 28406 • (910) 538-4076 • www.dramtreebooks.com

A World War that started in a colonial wilderness...

To the rest of the world it was called the Seven Years War. To the British colonists in North America, it came to be known as the French & Indian War. It was sparked when a young Virginia militia officer named George Washington fired on what he believed to be an attacking French force in western Pennsylvania, that turned out to be a delegation of French soldiers approaching the British and their Indian allies to parley. It took the British several years, thousands of troops, and a mountain of money to keep King George's subjects in the thirteen North American colonies speaking English instead of French. When it was all over, the king's ministers thought it only fair that the Americans help pay the costs of keeping them British.

Jumonville Glen in western Pennsylvania, the place where British militia stumbled into a fight with French emissaries and sparked a war in North America between Great Britain and France.

This image of a young George Washington was produced by Mount Vernon using modern forensic techniques.

America: The Jewel of the British Colonial Empire...

Before the war, England's colonies along the Atlantic seaboard of North America stretched from Spanish Florida to New France, what is now Canada. Each of the thirteen colonies developed independently of the others, and for different reasons. Some started for religious liberty. Some to provide a place for undesirables who were no longer welcome in their mother countries. Others were founded as part of a real estate scheme by men who helped King Charles II reclaim his crown in 1660. All of them were founded by people who sought to make their fortunes on a new continent with plenty of land and abundant natural resources.

With the American colonies separated from England by a wide Atlantic Ocean, it was impossible for London to keep a tight rein on their subjects half a world away. Questions and directives took weeks to travel from places like Virginia to England, and then more weeks to get an answer delivered in return. As a result, the American colonies began to govern themselves. Virginia's House of Burgesses was the first elected body for governing a colony, but they were soon followed in some shape or form by the other twelve. As long as the king received his taxes, and as long as the colonies stayed broadly in line with British colonial policy as practiced in the rest of the British empire, the Americans were allowed a great degree of freedom to set their own laws and rules. That policy, called salutary neglect, made relations between America and England contentious after the French & Indian War.

Stretching from Canada to Spanish Florida, the thirteen British colonies in North America were a source of wealth for the Mother Country, providing raw materials for British industry and markets for its finished goods.

The powers that the various colonies took upon themselves were, in most cases, assumed rather than delegated. Whether or not they had the blessing of Parliament, the colonies all took the position that they - and only they - had the right to directly tax their citizens. Some taxes, like customs duties and other measures designed to regulate trade, belonged to England. Direct taxes intended to raise revenue were reserved to the colonies. The colonial position on taxation was reinforced by their contention that they had no elected representatives in Parliament, and so had no voice in whether or not such taxes should be passed by the crown's ministers. It was, to the colonists' minds, taxation without representation. For their part, Parliament argued that as English colonies, the Americans were in a sense represented by Parliament as a whole, and so were subject to Parliament's rulings. Needless to say, the colonists did not agree with that assessment.

The distances separating Parliament (left) from its colonies in North America led to the colonists establishing their own governments in bodies like Virginia's House of Burgesses (above). That independence, or salutary neglect, would have consequences that later led to revolution.

The colonial economy was based on a system called **mercantilism**. Under this system, colonies existed to enrich the mother country (in this case, England). In places like North Carolina's Lower Cape Fear, colonists milked longleaf pine trees of the resin that was used to produce tar, pitch, and turpentine. These items, collectively called naval stores, were exported to England and used to keep Great Britain's merchant and naval fleets afloat. North Carolina was the largest source of those materials in the entire British empire. Things like timber, minerals, rice and other raw materials, were shipped to England and transformed into manufactured products like furniture, which was then sold back to the colonists. Under the mercantile system, the colonies not only provided raw materials for industry in England, but also provided markets for English businesses to sell finished products to.

Fighting a Costly War...

The Battle of the Monongahella (above) in the summer of 1755 was one of many bloody clashes the British fought to defend their colonial possessions in North America. The costs of the war left deep holes in the royal treasury that had to be repaid. Prime Minister George Grenville (right) saw a stamp tax as a way to repair Britain's depleted coffers.

Great Britain's debt doubled as a result of the French & Indian War. The interest on that debt was crippling, and King George's badly drained treasury needed a quick infusion of funds to begin paying it down. The fighting in America was just one theater of that conflict. England found itself fighting across the globe in a world war, and desperately needed to recoup the money spent on fending off the French king's armies in the American colonies. A stamp tax was proposed in March 1764 by the ministry of Lord George Grenville, who estimated it would produce as much as £60,000 a year. That money would not only help retire the debt of the French & Indian War, but would also help with the costs of keeping troops in America to protect their victory. Prime Minister Grenville realized the tax would be unpopular with the colonists, and invited them to suggest alternative ways of generating income for the government. But by the time he met with representatives of the colonists two months later, it was evident that the stamp tax was going to happen.

"Sons of Liberty" Resist...

The Stamp Act passed with only a few dissenters on March 22, 1765. Col. Isaac Barre, member of Parliament and veteran of the French & Indian War in the American colonies, spoke for the opposition when he warned that the American "Sons of Liberty" would oppose the measure. Barre noted that the Americans were jealous of their rights as Englishmen, and would not willingly submit to a direct tax they had no say in creating.

Barre's warnings were ignored. The stamp duty was scheduled to begin on November 1, 1765. In practice, it would impact every aspect of life in the colonies. The Stamp Act taxed all legal documents produced in the colonies, as well as all business documents, too. While those items might be expected to be taxed, the act went even further, going so far as to tax virtually every printed thing in the colonies. It was the first time Parliament placed a direct tax on the Americans. To the colonists, that was bad enough (though even at their peak, British taxes on the Americans were still smaller than those imposed on the king's subjects in England). Add in the colonial dislike of having an army of British redcoats stationed in their cities and towns, and the Americans were ripe for rebellion. In their minds, if Parliament was allowed to impose one such tax, more would undoubtedly follow.

A British four pence stamp

The things they taxed...

The list of things taxed by the Stamp Act was long. It included items like legal and business documents, newspapers, pamphlets, almanacs, playing cards, dice, insurance policies, ship's papers, deeds, diplomas, marriage certificates, and various other licenses issued by authorities in the colonies. If it was printed, it was required to carry the king's stamp, signifying that the tax had been paid.

Col. Isaac Barre

How taxes were paid in North Carolina...

In North Carolina, colonists never experienced a direct tax before the Stamp Act was passed. Colonies taxed their own citizens, then delivered a portion of the monies collected to the king's treasury. Those funds came in the form of land taxes called quitrents, poll taxes paid when one registered to vote, fees paid by ships carrying cargoes from one port to another, duties charged on imported items brought into the colony, and a tax on liquor.

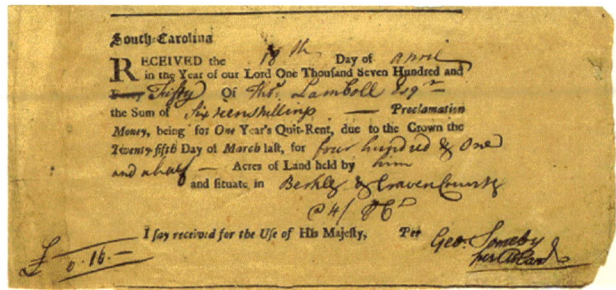

A quitrent receipt from South Carolina.

Salutary Neglect and a tradition of American freedom...

Frustration with Great Britain had been growing since the French & Indian War ended, caused in large part by taxes and new rules imposed on the colonies beginning in 1763. For nearly 150 years, the policy of salutary neglect had left the colonies to essentially rule themselves in most day to day matters. When Great Britain tried to tighten their grip on the colonies, they rebelled. Already issues like the king's Proclamation Line decree that prohibited settlement west of the Appalachian Mountains struck a sour note with settlers eager to seek their fortunes on the other side of that mountain range. Stricter trade regulations chaffed at the colonists too. When the Stamp Act was passed, colonial anger was widespread. Making matters worse, violators of the Stamp Act would not be tried in local courts with juries who knew them, but rather in Admiralty Courts in Nova Scotia without the benefit of any jury at all.

The House of Burgesses in Williamsburg, Virginia (above), was the first elective body where colonials in America sent their own representatives to pass laws and govern in the absence of British authority. The great distances between the colonies and London necessitated such a move. King George III (left) passed a law in 1763 that prohibited American settlers from encroaching on lands set aside for Native Americans west of the Appalachian Mountains.

"...a burthen too great for the circumstances of the Colonies to bear..."

Judge Maurice Moore, of Brunswick Town on the Cape Fear River, protested the Stamp Act in a pamphlet that spoke for a majority of North Carolinians outraged over the tax. "The Stamp Duty is itself a burthen too great for the circumstances of the Colonies to bear," he wrote, "considering the many restrictions that have been put upon their trade, which are at present vigorously enforced throughout America..." Parliament argued that Americans were represented by that body as a whole, with "virtual representation" that accounted for the best interests of both the colonies and the empire. Moore dismissed the notion, declaring "...it is a doctrine which only tends to allow the Colonists a shadow of that substance which they must ever be slaves without. It cannot surely be consistent with British liberty, that any set of men should represent another, detached from them in situation and interest, without the privity and consent of the represented." Moore's vocal opposition to the Stamp Act caused Royal Governor William Tryon to suspend him from his judgeship in 1766. Tryon attempted to dismiss the influence Judge Moore had, writing that "...he is a leading man in this river (the Cape Fear River) though he enjoys no great share of popularity in other parts of the province."

Judge Maurice Moore, Jr. of Brunswick Town (left) wrote a pamphlet arguing against the Stamp Act. It put him at odds with Royal Gov. William Tryon.

A conjectural drawing of Judge Moore's Brunswick Town home.

The ruins of Judge Moore's home at Brunswick Town.

The Declaration of Rights & Grievances

A month before the act was to become law, most of the thirteen colonies sent delegates to New York for the Stamp Act Congress. Only New Hampshire, Virginia, Georgia, and North Carolina were absent. North Carolina did not send representatives because Royal Governor William Tryon blocked the colony from sending any. But the colonists who did attend issued a plea for the hated act to be repealed. In a Declaration of Rights and Grievances, the colonists asserted their rights as Englishmen and rejected the stamp levy as taxation without representation. To show they were serious, delegates resolved that their colonies would refuse to import European goods, using economic might as a weapon to get the measure reversed. When even some of their own English merchants joined the Americans' call for repeal, Parliament finally listened. By March 1766, Parliament rescinded the Stamp Act, to the delight of the Americans. But between the October 1765 Stamp Act Congress and the repeal five months later, friction between Great Britain and its American colonies grew greater by the day.

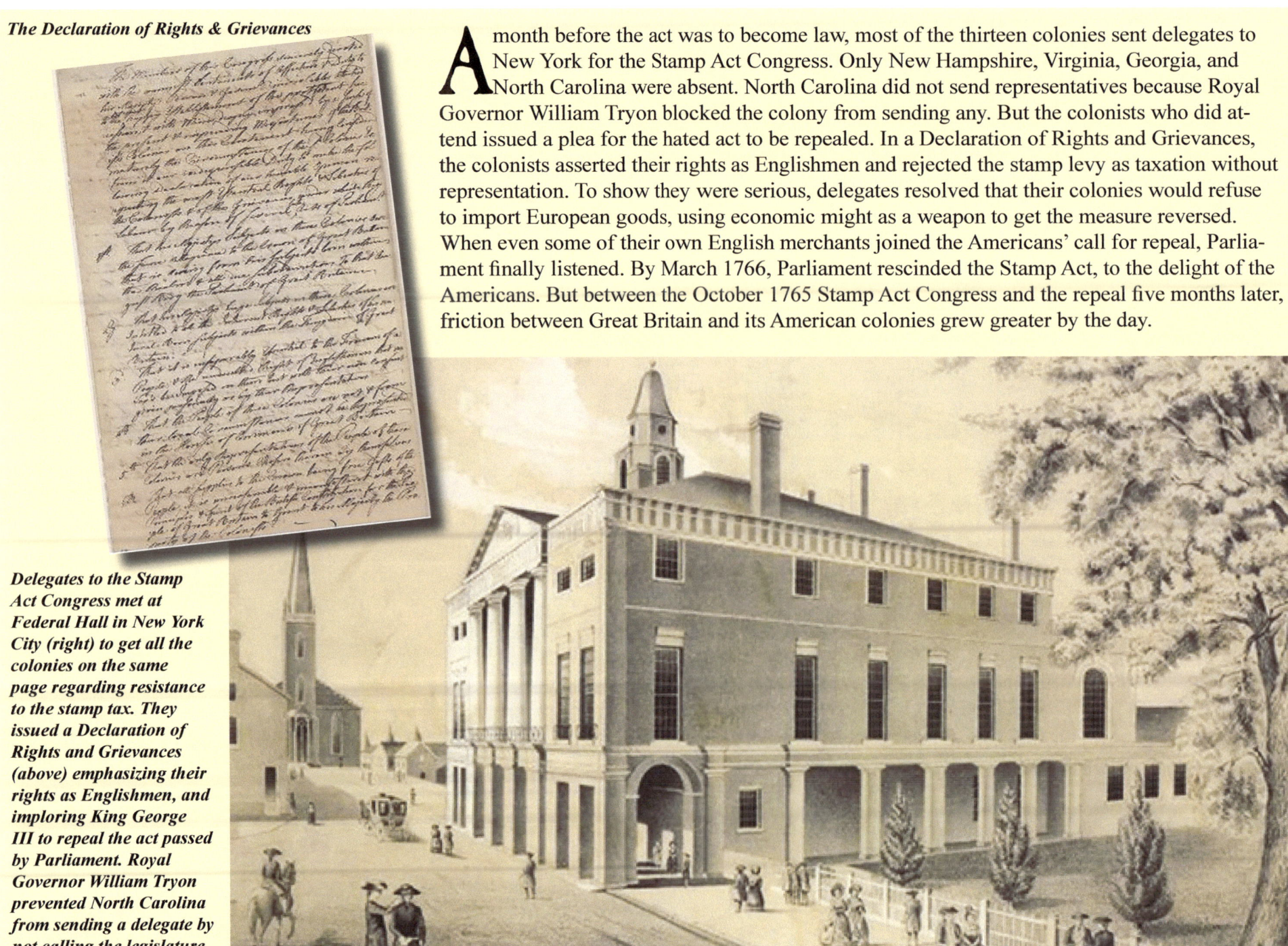

Delegates to the Stamp Act Congress met at Federal Hall in New York City (right) to get all the colonies on the same page regarding resistance to the stamp tax. They issued a Declaration of Rights and Grievances (above) emphasizing their rights as Englishmen, and imploring King George III to repeal the act passed by Parliament. Royal Governor William Tryon prevented North Carolina from sending a delegate by not calling the legislature into session.

"LIBERTY, PROPERTY, and NO STAMP DUTY! And CONFUSION TO LORD BUTE AND HIS ADHERENTS!"

John Stuart, 2nd Lord Bute

In the fall of 1765, a crowd of 500 Cape Fear men burned Lord Bute in effigy (right) in protest of the Stamp Act.

The biggest protests of the Stamp Act happened in seaports, home to the people who would be most impacted by the tax. In the summer and fall of 1765, North Carolinians grew more and more angry over the approaching November day when the Stamp Act would go into effect. By October, colonists in southeastern North Carolina were in no mood for compromise or reconciliation. Nearly 500 men gathered in Wilmington on October 19, twelve miles upriver from Brunswick, and expressed their displeasure by burning the effigy of a stamp tax supporter in tar barrels set alight for that purpose. Then the crowd went from house to house, gathering more men into their midst until at a bonfire they all drank toasts to "LIBERTY, PROPERTY, and NO STAMP DUTY! And CONFUSION TO LORD BUTE AND HIS ADHERENTS!" (The colonists incorrectly blamed Lord Bute, the former British Prime Minister, for the Stamp Act).

Two weeks later, on the night before the Stamp Act was to go into effect, another crowd of Wilmington men led a solemn funeral procession down Market Street for "Liberty," complete with a coffin, funeral procession, mourners, and a muffled drum that kept a slow and steady beat, while a death knell pealed from the town bell. At a grave dug for the purpose, the men paused. The coffin lid was opened, and the leaders discovered an ever so faint pulse in Liberty that gave them hope that there was still some life left in it. The crowd rejoiced, returned to a bonfire with the now rejuvenated Liberty seated in an armchair, and celebrated cheating death of their rights as Englishmen.

Who were the Sons of Liberty?

The Sons of Liberty took their name from a speech Col. Isaac Barre gave in Parliament that warned the British legislators that a stamp tax would not be well received in the American colonies. The group originated in Boston, Massachusetts in 1765. Exactly how they came to be is not entirely clear, but the organization's origins came from the growing discontent American colonials had with what they saw as unreasonable and overbearing actions by King George III's government.

Some origin stories have the Sons of Liberty evolving from the secret nighttime meetings held under the Liberty Tree by Boston's "secret nine," a group that included Samuel Adams and others who would, within the decade, become the most vocal opponents of British rule. The Boston Sons of Liberty are perhaps best known for staging the Boston Tea Party. Benjamin Franklin's "Join or Die" newspaper illustration emphasized the need for the colonies to work together to oppose the Stamp Act.

By the time of the Stamp Act Congress, other colonies began forming their own chapters of the group. Realizing that they must work in unison (or at least know what was happening in the other colonies), the Sons of Liberty were originally concerned mostly with establishing communications between the thirteen colonies as resistance to the Stamp Act grew and solidified.

On the Cape Fear, Sons of Liberty men like Cornelius Harnett, Jr. and Robert Howe became leaders of the opposition to the tax in North Carolina.

Boston Sons of Liberty, led by men like Samuel Adams, roused support for their anti-stamp tax positions through public displays against it. The notice to the right announces the resignation of a stamp official under Boston's Liberty Tree.

The Boston Tea Party (above), in which Sons of Liberty disguised as Native Americans dumped over 300 chests of British tea into the Charles River, may be the best known exploit of the group in Massachusetts.

Benjamin Franklin's "Join or Die" illustration.

"The Inhabitants immediately assembled about me & demanded a Categorical Answer whether I intended to put the Act relating (to) the Stamps in force. The Town Bell was rung(,) Drums (were) beating, Colours (were) flying and (a) great concourse of People (were) gathered together." - Dr. William Houston

Protesters in Wilmington demand Dr. Houston not enforce the Stamp Act.

The Stamp Act went into effect on November 1, 1765, but it took a few weeks longer before the first stamps made their way into Carolina waters at the end of the month. Meanwhile Dr. William Houston of Duplin County was, unknown to him, appointed Stamp Receiver. When Houston rode into Wilmington on November 16, he was confronted by a large crowd of angry citizens who made it clear they did not like the stamps or anyone involved with them. Dr. Houston, quick to read the mood of the crowd, hastily resigned his position as a stamp officer in front of the courthouse, declaring that he pledged to not "execute any Office disagreeable to the People of the province." As the ink dried on his resignation, the crowd of several hundred cheered and placed Houston in an armchair that they hoisted high on their shoulders, and paraded the physician around the town square. With Houston in tow, the crowd next stopped at Alexander Steuart's *Gazette* newspaper office to demand he resume printing his publication. Steuart had ceased publishing because of the cost of the tax the Stamp Act placed on his newspaper, but fearing that the mob might destroy his press if he refused their demand, he promised to do as they wished and begin printing again. The crowd, many of them wearing hats with the word LIBERTY decorating their crowns, proceeded to the nearby bonfire to celebrate their victories with toasts and cheers.

Credit Cards Not Accepted...

Concerns of the North Carolina men over the Stamp Act went beyond the political. The tax was to be paid in specie, meaning hard money like gold or silver. In the whole colony, and in the Lower Cape Fear especially, specie was hard to come by.

This artist's model of Bellfont, a.k.a. Russellborough, gives an idea of how grand a house it was. The home to two royal governors, its ruins (see below) can be viewed at Brunswick Town/Fort Anderson State Historic Site.

The King's Man in N.C. tries persuasion to get cooperation...

The ruins of Bellfont (Russellborough) at Brunswick Town

In the fall of 1765, Gov. William Tryon was ill and largely confined to his bed at Bellfont, just north of Brunswick Town. Nevertheless, he was concerned at the defiance people in North Carolina - especially on the Cape Fear - had for the Stamp Act. Such open hostility to the king's tax was not only unusual, but also skirted much too close to the line of sedition for Tryon's liking. Two days after Dr. William Houston was compelled to resign his position as Stamp Receiver, Tryon tried to persuade the men of the Cape Fear region to accept the stamp tax at a dinner for fifty leading men of the Cape Fear. Tryon was at his most gracious and sympathetic, but nevertheless duty bound to carry out London's orders regarding the stamps. The governor was hopeful that his persuasion would carry the day as the men filed out and made their way home.

The next day, the men returned and thanked Tryon for his concern for the colony, but respectfully declined his arguments in favor of the Stamp Act. The tax was, they insisted, a threat to the liberty of British subjects, asserting that "submission to any part of so oppressive and...so unconstitutional attempts, is opening a direct inlet for Slavery, which all Mankind will endeavor to avoid." Even when Tryon offered to pay a portion of the tax from his own pocket, the colonists declined. The Cape Fear men especially objected to the part of the Stamp Act that called for violators to be tried at admiralty courts in Nova Scotia, and not by juries of their peers.

The refusal put the royal governor in a difficult position. Tryon was not new to the colony, and he knew full well how stubborn the people of North Carolina could be. But he was also a Crown officer, and it was his duty to see that the Stamp Act was enforced. It was a tightrope he would have to find a way to walk. Nevertheless, when the hated stamps finally arrived on the Cape Fear aboard the British sloop *Diligence* on November 28, 1765, there was no stamp officer present to accept them. As a result, the stamps stayed aboard ship.

American colonists charged with Stamp Act crimes were to be taken to Halifax, Nova Scotia (above) for trial before an admiralty court.

*A model of **H.M.S. Diligence** by the Hampton Roads Ship Model Society.*

Admiralty Courts (above) differed from normal courts in that they were miitary courts, and judged cases using military rules. Americans objected to them in large part because such courts deprived them of a jury of their peers, neighbors who would likely have been more sympathetic to the person on trial.

"The mayor, aldermen, and other Gentlemen of Wilmington greeted Tryon at the Market Street wharf, and the New Hanover County regiment of militia lined the street leading from the dock to the house in which Tryon stayed. A discharge of seventeen pieces of artillery saluted the governor, and captains of ships in the harbor unfurled their colors."

Tryon's next opportunity to seek public support for the Stamp Act occurred in Wilmington on December 20 upon the ceremonial publication of his commission as governor of the province. Tryon arrived in North Carolina in 1764 as Lieutenant Governor, and assumed the governorship in 1765 upon the death of Arthur Dobbs. However, his gubernatorial commission arrived later in the year. Captain Constantine Phipps brought Tryon from Brunswick Town in his barge or dinghy "with all the parade peculiar to that kind of Gentry.... The mayor, aldermen, and other Gentlemen of Wilmington greeted Tryon at the Market Street wharf, and the New Hanover County regiment of militia lined the street leading from the dock to the house in which Tryon stayed. A discharge of seventeen pieces of artillery saluted the governor, and captains of ships in the harbor unfurled their colors." However, the pomp and pageantry quickly dissipated when Tryon, in his address, stressed "the Necessity of America's helping her Mother" and asked the people to receive the Stamps.

The crowd responded with a general hiss, which changed to a cheer when the captain of a merchant vessel raised the Irish national flag, apparently a tribute to the deceased governor Dobbs, a native of Ireland. Phipps moved to take the flag, which so infuriated the townspeople and militia that they threatened to burn the captain's small boat, probably the vessel used to bring Tryon to Wilmington, unless the colors were surrendered. After Phipps complied with their demand, the mob placed the flag in the boat, dragged it around town, and finally launched it. Following a harangue by an exasperated Tryon, the mob gathered around several barrels of punch and an ox that had been provided by the governor

Royal Governor Arthur Dobbs, who died at Brunswick Town. William Tryon replaced Dobbs as governor in 1765.

The new governor was saluted by seventeen cannon firing as he arrived in Wilmington.

for refreshments. They broke open the barrels and let the punch flow through the streets, put the head of the ox in a gallows, and gave the body to the slaves. But even the "Negroes disdained to taste the 'Bait of Slaven' which was [la]id for their Masters...." Phipps threatened to go to Brunswick Town and bring up the *Diligence* in order to blow the town to pieces.

    Wilmingtonians and those of the Lower Cape Fear successfully defied the governor, in part because the British lacked enough men to restrain the crowd. Sheriffs, constables, and municipal leaders all joined the protesters, rendering the governors position untenable, short of full-scale violence. Phipps never effected his threat to destroy Wilmington. And on behalf of Wilmington, mayor Moses John DeRosset attempted in part to exonerate the townspeople by asking Governor Tryon not to "lay the whole Blame of every Transaction relative to the Opposition made to the Stamp-Act on this Borough when it is so well known that the whole country has been equally concerned in it." The governor accepted the apology, declaring that he was "willing to

Elizabeth McKoy's model of colonial Wilmington, showing the foot of Market Street.

forget every Impropriety of Conduct" that the mayor, aldermen, and of Wilmington "have shown personally towards me in the late Commotions." Nevertheless, Tryon retaliated for the embarrassment by moving the seat of government to New Bern. When he arrived in North Carolina, Tryon apparently intended to make Wilmington the capital of the colony, and purchased Bellfont with that idea in mind. After the Wilmington debacle, the governor persuaded the legislature in 1766 to make New Bern the permanent capital and to build a magnificent statehouse and governor's residence in that town -Tryon Palace.

Tryon Palace in New Bern, N.C.

British boarding parties from H.M.S. Viper came aboard the merchant vessels Dobbs, Patience, *and* Ruby *to check their cargoes to see if they carried the stamps required by the act of Parliament (left). Though the ships were at sea before the Stamp Act went into effect, the ships were seized by British authorities anyway.*

The Cape Fear was the only port in British North America where the tax stamps were never landed, but that was an outcome that was only revealed later. In the early days of 1766, Governor Tryon was still trying to find a way to get North Carolinians to accept the stamp tax; while the people of the colony were equally hard at work trying to resist it. Tryon had two sloops of war at his disposal if he needed them, *H.M.S. Diligence*, commanded by Capt. Constantine Phipps, and *H.M.S. Viper*, under Capt. Jacob Lobb. On January 14, two sloops arrived in the Cape Fear River carrying unstamped papers, setting the scene for the next act of the crisis. The *Dobbs*, from the Caribbean island of St. Christopher, and the *Patience*, from Philadelphia, had both put to sea before the Stamp Act actually went into effect, leaving them no way to comply with the new law even if they wanted to. Upon arrival, both ships were seized by *H.M.S. Viper*. Not long after, a third ship, the *Ruby*, was also seized.

The seizures had an immediate crippling effect on the maritime trade of the Cape Fear. Ships that would likely have called on the ports at Wilmington and Brunswick veered off for other harbors to avoid sailing into the clutches of Lobb and the British navy. One report from Wilmington said, "The trade of this river is at present entirely ruined! Besides the three vessels that have been seized by the man of war, seven others have, within a fortnight past, put into our capes; but on hearing of the above-mentioned seizures, made off for other ports. This is a stroke that must be felt by the people of Cape Fear, as these ten vessels would have carried off a vast deal of tar and turpentine, which, in a few weeks, will be running through our streets."

This model at the Hampton Roads Maritime Museum is of a British sloop of war. H.M.S. Viper would have looked similar to this.

> "Where is your late boasted Courage and resolution? Have the Wilmingtonians, Brunswickers, and New-Hanovarians lost their senses and their souls, and are they determined to tamely submit to slavery?" —Wilmington Gazette, 1765

Wary of the wrath of the people, Capt. Lobb turned the ship's papers of the *Dobbs* and *Patience* over to port collector William Dry, who forwarded the documents to North Carolina Attorney General Robert Jones, for an opinion as to whether or not the case should be prosecuted further. In a blow to the local resistance, Jones ruled the seizures were legitimate and that both ships should be delivered to Halifax, Nova Scotia for trial before an admiralty court.

Infuriated, the people of Wilmington and Brunswick refused to provide provisions to resupply *H.M.S. Viper*. An anonymous letter in the *Wilmington Gazette* newspaper shamed the pride of the Cape Fear men, asking "Where is your late boasted Courage and resolution? Have the Wilmingtonians, Brunswickers, and New-Hanovarians lost their senses and their souls, and are they determined to tamely submit to slavery?" When Jones' ruling became known, William Dry received a letter signed by forty fellow citizens, warning him against releasing the two ships' papers to the British for their removal to Nova Scotia and trial. The letter said "...very ill Consequences...will attend this affair..." Dry was alarmed, but as a man who took his oath of office seriously, he assured Gov. Tryon that he would release the papers if he was ordered to do so. To the neighbors that had written the warning letter, he replied that if he surrendered his post he might be replaced with a new Collector of Customs who would be much less sympathetic to the colonists' cause.

A bottle seal dated 1766 belonging to Port Collector William Dry (above), and his grave at Brunswick Town (left). Dry passed the decision on the legality of the ship seizures on the Cape Fear to Attorney General Robert Jones (below).

The NORTH CAROLINA GAZETTE:

The Cape Fear's first newspaper

The *North Carolina Gazette* was the first locally produced, widely circulated newspaper in the Cape Fear region. James Davis of New Bern was the colony's first printer, followed by Irishman Andrew Steuart of Philadelphia and later, Adam Boyd. Steuart relocated to Wilmington by early 1764 and made his living primarily by printing for the government. During the Stamp Act crisis, the *North Carolina Gazette* chronicled the resistance to the tax along the Cape Fear. The press used to produce it would have been very similar to the one pictured below.

This early printing press is one of the oldest in N.C., preserved at the Wachovia Historical Society Museum.

Confronting Governor Tryon...

Cornelius Harnett, Jr. and other Cape Fear Sons of Liberty marched on Royal Gov. William Tryon's home north of Brunswick to demand Tryon turn over the officers of the sloops of war that had seized the merchant vessels Dobbs, Patience, *and* Ruby.

Artificial Intelligence created this image of the angry crowd at Russellborough to confront Gov. Tryon. For a more accurate depiction of the governor's mansion, see the model on page 12.

Dry's reasoning did not impress the men of the Cape Fear. On February 18, 1766, the protestors decided a more forceful demonstration of their resolve was in order. Adopting the name Sons of Liberty, the men swore to prevent the Stamp Act from being enforced. The next day, almost 1,000 men from New Hanover, Brunswick, Bladen, and Duplin Counties marched to Tryon's home north of Brunswick. Among them was the Wilmington mayor, the town aldermen, and other men of note. At Bellfont (Russellborough) the following day, George Moore and Cornelius Harnett presented a letter to Tryon from Speaker of the Assembly John Ashe that guaranteed the royal governor's safety by informing him that his home and person would be guarded by armed members of the Sons of Liberty. The letter assured Gov. Tryon that the colonials only had a problem with the naval officers from the *Viper* and *Diligence* that were trying to enforce the stamp tax. The men believed Capt. Lobb was inside the governor's house and demanded to see him. Tryon was outraged at the suggestion. Nevertheless, when the main body of colonists withdrew from Tryon's lawn, 150 men remained to keep an eye on him. Violence was averted when word came that the British naval officer was, in fact, aboard the *Viper*.

As night fell, Gov. Tryon worried that the mob outside his door could move to seize the cannons at Fort Johnston, eleven miles south of Brunswick at the mouth of the river. If they did, it was unlikely Capt. John Dalrymple, commander of the small garrison of soldiers manning the fort, could stop them. Tryon sent orders to Capt. Phipps and his ship, *H.M.S. Diligence*, to reposition off the fort and take whatever steps deemed necessary to keep the fort and its guns in British hands.

Fort Johnston: Sentinel of the Cape Fear

N.C.'s first fort, named after an early governor and located at what is now modern Southport, played a crucial role in the Stamp Act and the Revolutionary War that followed it a decade later

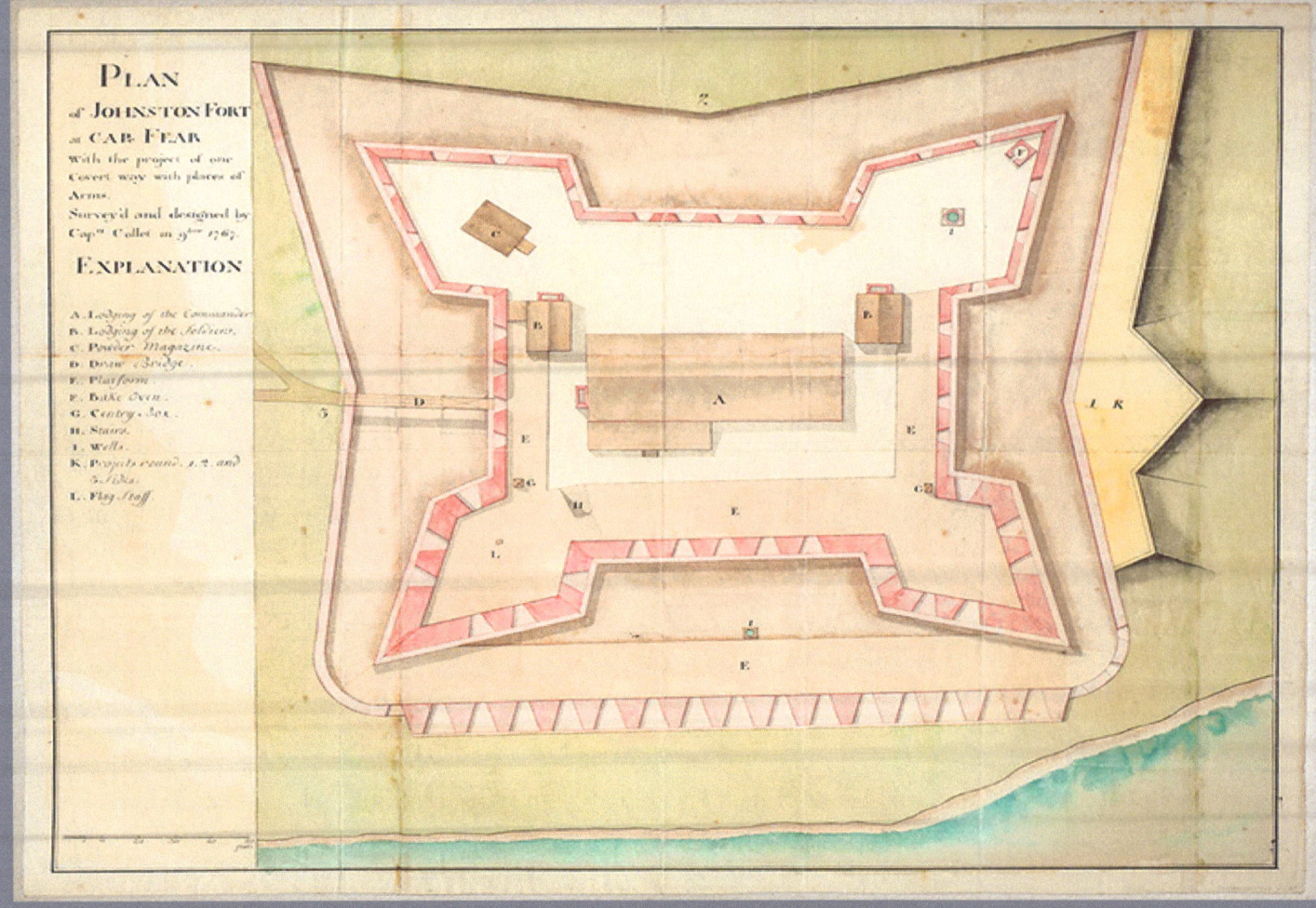

The plans for Fort Johnston as originally envisioned. The fort never achieved this level of development.

Construction started on the fort at the mouth of the Cape Fear River in 1748 under the administration of Royal Governor Arthur Dobbs. At the time, the fledgling settlements at Smithville (modern Southport) and Wilmington were vulnerable to attack by Spanish marauders who preyed on English shipping and settlements along the eastern seaboard. In fact, even as construction began, Spanish raiders sailed past the fort in the fall of 1748 to attack Brunswick Town farther upriver, looting the settlement and carting off slaves who had gathered at St. Philip's Church for Sunday services.

By 1765, the fort was operational, though it never achieved the size and form envisioned in the original plans seen at left. Fort Johnston served as a key strategic site on the Cape Fear during the Revolutionary War, for both the British and the rebellious Americans a decade later. The fort was burned by American forces in 1775, but was reoccupied later.

Until it was decommissioned in 2004, the fort was the oldest serving U.S. military installation in the United States.

Phipps dispatched an officer and five men with tools to spike the Fort Johnston cannons to prevent their capture. At Brunswick, some of the armed Sons of Liberty kicked in the door of William Dry's house and rifled his desk to find the papers of the sloops *Dobbs* and *Patience*. After pausing to decide their next move, 300 men under Col. Hugh Waddell marched to take the fort. Capt. Lobb, learning of the colonist's intentions, realized that the *Viper* was unable to navigate the treacherous Cape Fear to lend assistance to Dalrymple and Phipps. There were no river pilots available to show them the way. He dispatched a message to Phipps ordering the fort cannons spiked to prevent their capture.

Cape Fear Men Try To Reason With A Viper...

On the morning of February 20, a delegation of protestors climbed into rowboats and headed for a meeting with Capt. Lobb aboard the *Viper*. The men demanded the British release the three captured merchant sloops, but Lobb deferred, saying he needed time to consult with Gov. Tryon. By noon William Dry and a vice admiralty judge Thomas McGuire joined Capt. Lobb and Capt. Phipps aboard the *Diligence* to plot what to do next. Tryon left the noon meeting believing his intentions were known to Lobb and Dry. The governor authorized the release of the *Ruby*, but intended that the *Dobbs* and *Patience* be sent to Halifax to have their fate decided. Lobb, especially, was adamant that the *Patience* remain in British custody. Time and persuasion must have changed his mind, because by that evening both of the remaining sloops had been released. The fact that more and more armed men filtered into Brunswick from surrounding counties also probably influenced Lobb's decision. The captain decided the status of the merchant ships would be decided when the surveyor general of customs arrived to consider the matter. Until then, the ports of North Carolina would remain open.

A delegation of Cape Fear men rowed out to H.M.S. Viper (above) to try and convince Capt. Jacob Lobb to release the impounded merchant ships taken for Stamp Act violations.

Spiking Ft. Johnston's Guns...

Fearing that angry protestors would take the cannons of Fort Johnston, Gov. Tryon orderd the guns be spiked to prevent them from being able to fire. This was done by hammering a nail or some other piece of iron into the touch hole of the cannons. The fort had a collection of eight 18pdrs, eight 9pdrs, and 23 swivel guns. Capt. Phipps realized the danger if the guns fell into the hands of the protestors and dispatched men to disable them.

The sculpture, **Spiking the Guns at Whitehaven.**

The King's Stamp Man Takes Refuge with the Governor...

That evening, Governor Tryon opened his door at Bellfont to find William Pennington on his porch. The Comptroller of Customs sought refuge with Tryon from the protestors who were scouring the area to find him. The governor graciously admitted the king's officer, offering him a bed for the night.

Around eight in the morning on February 21, Col. James Moore appeared at Bellfont leading a small group of men. Before Tryon could stop them, Moore and his fellows had seized Pennington and were leading him away from the governor's porch. Tryon called out for them to stop, informing Moore and the men that Pennington was engaged in official business and enjoyed the Crown's protection while he did it. Tryon declared the stamp officer could not be taken. Moore sized up the situation, and departed. Within five minutes, the roads and driveways around Bellfont were filled with armed men.

After successfully convincing Capt. Lobb to release the three captive sloops, the protestors felt they could add another success at the governor's house. Around ten that night, Cornelius Harnett led a detachment of about 60 men to the house and sent a note to Tryon. It declared that the citizens only wanted to talk to the stamp officer, and promised that Pennington would not be harmed. But the protestors added that, in the event the stamp officer did not come out, then they could not prevent any bad consequences that might happen. Tryon again refused to send Pennington out, but did say that anyone who wished to speak to him was welcome to come inside and do so. Tryon again refused to turn Pennington over to the colonials. Harnett threatened to remove Pennington by force if necessary.

Watching this discussion, Pennington told the governor that it might be better all around if he just went with the locals. Tryon was reluctant, but in order to avoid violence, finally agreed. But before he would let Pennington step outside to meet his fate with Harnett and

Gov. Tryon offers Pennington a place to stay at Russellborough.

his men, Tryon forced Pennington to resign his commission. In doing so, Tryon actually avoided having to charge the protestors with insulting a king's officer, an offense with steep penalties. Pennington left Bellfont with Cornelius Harnett, and the entire group of men retired to Brunswick.

By the flickering of torchlight at the colonial port, the armed men surrounded Pennington. He was joined in the circle by the port collector, William Dry. The two men sized up the situation and, at Harnett's prompting, made an oath that they would never, directly or indirectly, issue any stamped paper. Town clerks and lawyers present were required to swear the same. Once everyone in a position of responsibility regarding the stamps had complied, the mob broke up and everyone went home. The protestors had notched another victory against the stamp tax. A newspaper in Virginia noted the Cape Fear men's success, writing "It is well worthy of observation that few instances can be produced of such a number of men being together so long, and behaving so well; not the least noise or disturbance, nor any person seen disguised with liquor, during the whole time of their stay at Brunswick; neither was there any

"It is well worthy of observation that few instances can be produced of such a number of men...behaving so well;...nor any person seen disguised with... liquor, during the whole time of their stay at Brunswick; neither was there any injury offered to any person, but the whole affair conducted with decency and spirit..."

— *Virginia Gazette*

injury offered to any person, but the whole affair conducted with decency and spirit, worthy of the imitation of all the Sons of Liberty throughout the Continent."

After things settled down, Gov. Tryon was remarkably calm about the whole episode. Only two men were removed from their jobs in retaliation. Judge Maurice Moore was removed from the Superior Court, and newspaper man Alexander Steuart was ordered to stop printing. Moore had offended the government with his pamphlet against the Stamp Act, and Steuart was deemed guilty of printing an "inflammatory" letter in his *Gazette* newspaper.

William Pennington resigns as Stamp Comptroller at the Brunswick tavern, as protestors look on.

Leaders of the protest, later leaders of the Revolution...

Cornelius Harnett, Jr. and Hugh Waddell were leaders of the Sons of Liberty in the Lower Cape Fear. Harnett was born in Chowan Precinct in 1723, but by 1726 had relocated with his family to Brunswick on the Cape Fear River. A merchant and farmer, Harnett owned Maynard (later named Hilton) plantation at the site of the Sweeny Water Teatment Plant in modern Wilmington, as well as Poplar Grove plantation in modern Scotts Hill. Harnett served his community in several positions including justice of the peace and in the General Assembly. He became increasingly involved with the debate over whether or not the colonies should break away from Great Britain, and by the 1770s was a leading figure in the movement. Captured in Onslow County by the British in 1781, he was brought back to occupied Wilmngton in April of that year, where he died in captivity. His grave is visible from the sidewalk next to the graveyard at St. James Episcopal Church at Fourth and Market Streets in Wilmington.

Irishman Hugh Waddell served under James Innes at Fort Cumberland in the French & Indian War, helped build Fort Dobbs near Statesville, N.C., led militia against the Cherokees, and as a general led troops under Gov. William Tryon in the Regulator Rebellion. Waddell served as a delegate from Bladen County in the N.C. General Assembly, and had extensive business connections with his brother-in-law, merchant John Burgwin. He died after a long illness at Fort Johnston in 1773.

Col. Hugh Waddell

A London cartoon from 1766 mourning the end of the Stamp Act

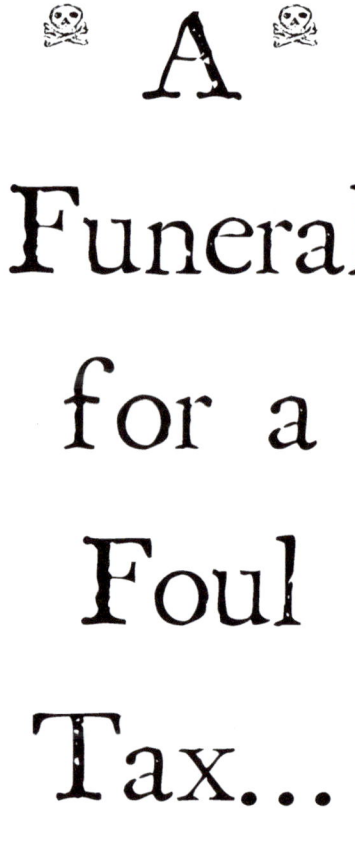

A Funeral for a Foul Tax...

In March 1766, Parliament repealed the Stamp Act, avoiding the very real potential for violence that could have occurred if they had not. The protests on the Cape Fear, with colonists challenging the authority of crown officers and the royal governor in his own front yard, were ample evidence of that. In the aftermath of the resistance to the stamp tax, life returned to something close to normal. By July, Capt. John Dalrymple died at his Fort Johnston post at the mouth of the Cape Fear River. In August, Gov. Tryon picked a local man, Robert Howe, to replace him as commander of Fort Johnston, at least temporarily. Howe held a commission as an associate district judge and as chief baron of the exchequer, so Tryon was well familiar with him.

By November 1766 Howe had already secured funds from the N.C. General Assembly to transfer the cannons guarding Wilmington to Fort Johnston. He immediately began a program to repair and fortify the shabby fort and turn it into something worthy of the name. Nevertheless, Howe would only command Fort Johnston for about a year. In November 1767, Capt. John Abraham Collet arrived with a commission that replaced him as the fort's commander. Both Howe and Collet would play major roles in the upcoming Revolutionary War on the Cape Fear less than a decade later.

Capt. John Abraham Collet and his Time on the Cape Fear

Swiss by birth, John Abraham Collet (sometimes spelled Collett) adopted a soldier's life by serving in the French army during the Seven Years War. Next came four years of education in map making and engineering, all of which served him well when he sought a commission in the British army. That commission was granted, and he received orders to assume command of Fort Johnston on the Cape Fear River in 1767.

Collet presented his commission to Royal Governor William Tryon at Brunswick in May of that year, displacing Robert Howe, the local planter who had been commanding the shabby little fort until that time. Howe was relegated to the post of second in command, as Collet's orders and regular army commission superceded Howe's claim to the job.

"That hopeful youth made a Bonfire of a country house of mine." - William Hooper

Collet served as aide-de-camp to Tryon when the governor marched on Hillsborough a year later to quell Regulator unrest there. While at the fort, Collet endeavored to produce an accurate map of North Carolina to bring it in line with a government edict requiring such maps from all of the American colonies. Collet based his map on an earlier work by William Churton, who passed away before he could finish it. Collet traveled to England to present it to the government, and did not return to N.C. until 1773. Upon returning, he undertook to repair and upgrade Fort Johnston, largely at his own expense.

By 1775, Collet was distrusted by the people of the Cape Fear. That July, his former second in command, Robert Howe, led 500 men to seize the fort and its supplies of cannon and powder. Collet evacuated to Boston, but returned in 1776 with Gen. Clinton's expedition. While once again on the Cape Fear, he led raiding parties that destroyed the homes of Whig leaders William Dry, Declaration of Independence signer William Hooper, and former comrade turned enemy Robert Howe.

A portion of Collet's N.C. map showing the mouth of the Cape Fear River.

The Rebellious, Rascally Robert Howe...

Robert Howe came from Carolina royalty, the son of Job Howe(s) of Charleston, and a mother who was a direct descendant of Sir John Yeamans, the Bajan sugar planter who became the first governor of Carolina back when it was all one colony in 1664.

Robert was born in 1732, after Job and Sarah Howe relocated to the Cape Fear.

Educated in England, Howe gained a reputation as a womanizer, and had at least six children of his own, not all of them legitimate. But one thing Howe did excel at was soldiering. He began his military career as a captain of the Bladen County militia in 1755, and parleyed that into political office, serving as Justice of the Peace in Bladen County, and in the N.C. General Assembly for both Bladen and Brunswick Counties in the 1760s.

During the French & Indian War, Howe served with Virginia troops before returning to N.C. to act as Gov. William Tryon's chief of artillery during the Regulator Rebellion. Howe commanded Fort Johnston on the Cape Fear River first from 1766-1767, then again from 1769-1773. In between, he served as second in command of the fort after Capt. John Abraham Collet displaced him from the top job.

As relations between Great Britain and its colonies soured in the 1770s, Robert Howe became an active leader of the Wilmington and Brunswick Committees of Safety, spearheading relief efforts for Boston after the British imposed an embargo on the rebellious New England city in the summer of 1774. After the battle at Lexington and Concord in April, 1775, Howe assumed command of the Cape Fear's militia and began training them up for war. In July of that year, he led 500 men against his former comrade in arms, John Abraham Collet, to take Fort Johnston from the British.

When N.C. raised its first two regiments of the Continmental Line in 1776, Robert Howe was given command of the First Regiment, and saw service with them at the Battle of Great Bridge in Norfolk, Virginia. That year he was promoted to the rank of general by the Continental Congress, and proceeded to see action in Florida, Georgia, and South Carolina. A lack of cooperation from the governor of Georgia, and political backbiting from factions in South Carolina, made Howe's tenure less than a complete success. It also contributed to his being blamed for the loss of Savannah, though a court martial cleared him of any culpability. Howe was next assigned to New York and West Point, and presided over the court martial and execution of British spy Maj. John Andre.

Robert Howe died at his plantation home in Bladen County in 1786, after having risen to the rank of Major General, making him the highest ranking Southern officer in George Washington's army.

Capt. John Abraham Collet delivering his commission and orders to take command of Fort Johnston to Robert Howe.

The End of the Stamp Act was not the end of British taxes...

The death of the Stamp Act did not mean the British were finished with taxing the American colonies. The Townshend Acts, passed in 1767, placed tariffs (taxes) on the importation of lead, glass, paint, paper, and tea. Once again the colonists resisted by refusing to import those things, hoping their abstinence would force Parliament to reconsider. It had worked with the Stamp Act, after all. But the Americans were never quite able to achieve the same unanimity of purpose for those later taxes that they had with the Stamp Act. Even so, on the Cape Fear at least, associations were established between local committees formed to resist what they saw as British tyranny, joining like-minded groups elsewhere. Cornelius Harnett wrote to the Sons of Liberty in South Carolina that, "We beg leave to assure you, that the inhabitants...are convinced of the necessity of adhering strictly to their former resolutions, and you may depend, they are as tenacious of their just rights as any of their brethren on the continent, and firmly resolved to stand or fall with them in support of the common cause of American liberty."

Penelope Barker and the ladies of Edenton, N.C. (right) sign a pledge to not buy or use British tea in response to the Townshend Act's taxation of the beverage, at the time the most popular drink in the American colonies. The boycott of tea comtributed to the growth in the popularity of coffee in the colonies.

First in Freedom from the First...

The Stamp Act contributed greatly to the American colonies finding common ground amongst themselves in defense of what they saw as their liberties, first as Englishmen, and later, as Americans. Those ties between the thirteen colonies would form the foundation of the networks that would come together a few short years later when the decision was made to break free of British rule once and for all. The Stamp Act resistance in North Carolina and on the Cape Fear River was certainly among the first rebellions against British rule in the American colonies. When Cape Fear men lined the banks of the river and refused to allow the hated stamps to be landed, they did so eight years before the much more famous Boston Tea Party - and they did it without the benefit of war paint and feathers to hide their identities. That the people of North Carolina rose up and successfully resisted the Stamp Act showed that from the very start, North Carolina has always been "First in Freedom."

The first page of the William Davie copy of the Mecklenburg Resolves in the Southern History Collection of the University of North Carolina

Glossary

Here are some words in this book that you may not be familiar with:

Forensic - (1) relating to, connected with, or used in courts of law, especially with reference to the scientific analysis of evidence. (2) relating, adapted, or suited to argumentation or to public discussion and debate; rhetorical.

Salutary - promoting or conducive to some beneficial purpose.

Quitrent - rent paid by a freeholder or copyholder in lieu of services that might otherwise have been required.

Decree - a formal and authoritative order, especially one having the force of law.

Privity - participation in the knowledge of something private or secret, especially as implying concurrence or consent.

Consent - to permit, approve, or agree; comply or yield.

Conjectural - given to making conjectures.

Reconciliation - the act of coming to an understanding and putting an end to hostility, as when former enemies agree to an amicable truce.

Effigy - a crude representation of someone disliked, used for purposes of ridicule.

Specie - coined money; coin.

Sedition - incitement of discontent or rebellion against a government; any action, especially in speech or writing, promoting such discontent or rebellion.

Admiralty Court - a military court under the authority of the British navy that did not require the same rights be afforded to the accused as civil courts did.

Peer(s) - a person who is equal to another in abilities, qualifications, age, background, and social status.

Gubenatorial - relating to a governor or the office of a governor.

Harangue - (n) a lengthy and aggressive speech; (v) to lecture (someone) at length in an aggressive and critical manner.

Untenable - something that is not able to be maintained or defended against attack or objection.

Exonerate - to absolve (someone) from blame for a fault or wrongdoing, especially after due consideration of the case.

Womanizer - a man who is promiscuous and often viewed negatively for their behavior, particularly in the context of romantic relationships.

Abstinence - the fact or practice of restraining oneself from indulging in something.

To Learn More About the Stamp Act and the Revolutionary War in the Cape Fear, try these titles by Dram Tree Books (www.dramtreebooks.com)

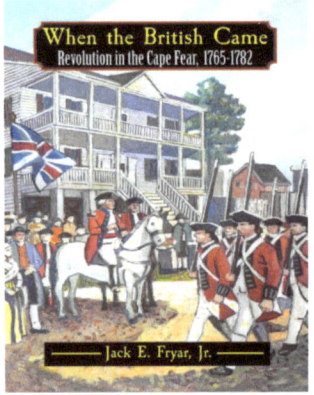

When the British Came: Revolution in the Cape Fear, 1765-1782
by Jack E. Fryar, Jr. (9780981460352 Hardcover $39.95/ 9780981460376 Paperback $29.95)

An encyclopedic history of the American Revolution as it happened in southeastern North Carolina. From the Stamp Act resistance, to the Regulator Rebellion, to the battle at Moores Creek, to the British occupation of Wilmington, this book has it all.

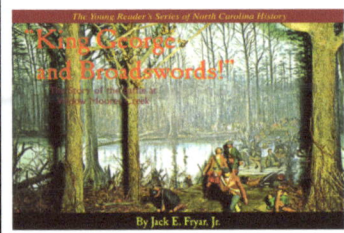

"King George and Broadswords!" The Battle at Widow Moores Creek
by Jack E. Fryar, Jr.. • 9780978624828

Also a title in the Young Readers Series of North Carolina History, this book introduces readers to the brief but violent and decisive victory of N.C. patriots over loyalist Highlanders in the 1776 battle that took place 23 miles northwest of Wilmington.

Revolutionary Incidents: Sketches of Character, Chiefly in the Old North State Vols. I & II
by E.W. Carruthers; edited by Jack E. Fryar, Jr.

A firsthand account of the American Revolution in North Carolina from the men and women who experienced it.

About the Author...

Jack E. Fryar, Jr. is a life-long resident of southeastern North Carolina, born and raised in Wilmington. He has been a professional writer and publisher since 1994. In 2000, he founded Dram Tree Books, a small publishing house whose titles tell the story of North Carolina and the Carolina coast. Jack has authored or edited thirty-two volumes of North Carolina and Cape Fear history, and is a frequent lecturer for historic groups in the region. His historical specialty is colonial North Carolina. Jack has served as a United States Marine, taught high school history, worked as a broadcaster, freelance magazine writer, sports announcer, and book designer. He holds Masters degrees in History and in Teaching from the University of North Carolina Wilmington.

www.ingramcontent.com/pod-product-compliance
Lightning Source LLC
Chambersburg PA
CBHW041457040426
42446CB00004B/231